SPECIAL **People** EDITION

DIANA, CHARLES AND *CAMILLA*

THE UNTOLD STORY OF
THE LOVE TRIANGLE THAT CHANGED
THE FUTURE OF THE MONARCHY

WINDSOR CASTLE

Always something there to remind us: Behind a commemorative Charles & Camilla mug at a Windsor shop, Diana looms on a souvenir plate.

CONTENTS

Barely two years on the job, Meghan, Duchess of Sussex (in 2019), gave up her royal duties and left the U.K. Top right: The Duchess of Windsor, formerly Wallis Simpson (in Givenchy), in 1954, nearly 20 years after her husband's abdication.

THE WOMEN WHO SHOOK THE THRONE

HOW EACH WINDSOR WIFE CHALLENGES THE ROYAL FAMILY'S TRADITIONS

From the moment guests arrived in St. George's Chapel at Windsor Castle on May 19, 2018, it was obvious that the wedding about to begin would be unlike any in British history. In the pews George and Amal Clooney and Serena Williams mixed with the Archbishop of Canterbury and Princess Mabereng Seeiso of Lesotho.

Never before had the rousing voices of a multicultural gospel choir filled the Gothic stone walls, or had an African-American preacher from Washington, D.C., delivered a passionate sermon from the pulpit. (The reception that night was surely the first on the premises deejayed by Idris Elba.) As Harry, the son of Princess Diana and Prince Charles, and Meghan Markle, the daughter of a television lighting director father and yoga instructor mother, debuted as husband and wife, those who lined the carriage route and watched on their phones around the world had reason to believe they were witnessing the House of Windsor renovated for a new era. But those who focused on the novelty of the new Duchess of Sussex being a biracial American did not anticipate the far bigger change the former TV star would bring to the monarchy. Driven, in part, by U.K. press coverage that ranged from intrusive to racist, she and Harry and their infant son Archie moved first to Canada, then to L.A. in early 2020 after renouncing their royal

'HER ELEVATED FASHION SENSE AND DEFT COMMUNICATION SKILLS MADE DIANA THE INFLUENCER IN CHIEF FOR THE YOUNGER GENERATION OF ROYALS'

duties. Not even the Queen saw it coming.

One of the reasons the British monarchy remains perennially fascinating to Americans is its timelessness, its ancient rituals and traditions. Yet change does happen behind palace doors, often sweeping in with new additions to the family. In the 1930s the arrival of American socialite Wallis Simpson led to a disruption of the status quo still felt today. Witty and elegant, Simpson charmed the future monarch Edward VIII, who was determined to make her his wife. But as the titular head of the Church of England, a king was forbidden from marrying a divorcée whose former spouse was alive. (Simpson had two living ex-husbands.) So Edward abdicated the throne, left England and married the woman he loved. As a result, Elizabeth II, the eldest daughter of Edward's brother, now sits on the throne—one of the world's longest-reigning and most popular monarchs.

Simpson wasn't the first bride and won't be the last to alter the course of history. Lady Diana Spencer, the shy former school aide—who struck the word "obey" from the customary vows when she wed Prince Charles in 1981—grew so popular that she threatened to overshadow the public profiles of the rest of Britain's ruling dynasty. Her concern for marginalized people, including AIDS patients, and her elevated fashion sense and deft communication skills made her the influencer in chief for a younger generation of royals, reshaping the role they play in society today.

At the same time, behind the scenes Diana proved to have a very different, destabilizing effect on what the royals call the Firm. Like her sister-in-law Sarah, Duchess of York, who married Prince Andrew in 1986, Diana was initially greeted by the family as a welcome infusion of spirit and modern style. (For "Fergie," as the former Sarah Ferguson was known, it was a short trip in the press from "breath of fresh air" to scandal magnet; she and Andrew split in 1992.)

When Diana's marriage

Windsor wives Sarah, HRH the Duchess of York, and Diana, HRH the Princess of Wales (at Epsom Derby in 1987), developed a close bond.

to Charles began to sour, she emerged as victor in the war of words fought by the estranged couple in the tabloid press. The damage to her husband's reputation and also to the larger family's was long-lasting. At the height of the so-called War of the Waleses, Diana revealed during a shockingly candid BBC interview in 1995 that her husband seemed never to have fallen out of love with a former girlfriend, Camilla Parker Bowles, once deemed an improper match for him by the older Windsors. Diana also wondered aloud if Charles was fit for the "suffocating" role that awaited him as King; polls found that many Britons agreed with her.

But in the ensuing years, Charles pulled off a neat trick: He not only wed the woman whom Diana called the third person in their marriage, he convinced the public that his former mistress could be their Queen. Perhaps this is the change Camilla brought when she wed into the Firm in 2005—the idea that it is never too late in life to marry for love.

In this special edition of *People,* we revisit what was the biggest story of its day: the love triangle of a future King, his longtime lover and the princess bride who longed to be the Queen of people's hearts. There hasn't been a scandal like it since, perhaps because younger royals, like Princes William and Harry, can now follow their own hearts. The British monarchy does evolve, but slowly.

Prince Charles at an inauguration ceremony for the Royal Regiment at Cardiff Castle in Cardiff, Wales, June 1969.

PART ONE

THE BACHELOR PRINCE

AT 22, CHARLES MET CAMILLA SHAND. THEIR AFFAIR DIDN'T LAST—SHE MARRIED ANOTHER MAN—LEAVING THE FUTURE KING ONE OF THE WORLD'S MOST ELIGIBLE MEN

ALL THE GIRLS HE LOVED BEFORE

THE PRINCE OF WALES ENJOYED A LONG BACHELORHOOD, INCLUDING AN EARLY, PASSIONATE LOVE FOR A WOMAN MOST ROYAL WATCHERS BELIEVED COULD NEVER BE QUEEN

IN 1974 PRINCE CHARLES'S GREAT-UNCLE AND MENTOR Lord Louis "Dickie" Mountbatten wrote him a letter with some advice: "I believe in a case like yours, the man should sow his wild oats and have as many affairs as he can before settling down." He may have had in mind keeping Charles single long enough for Mountbatten's teen granddaughter Amanda Knatchbull to come of age. (Knatchbull turned down Charles's proposal in 1979.) But he was also sending Charles another message: that his someday bride—a future Queen of England—could not herself have a history of oats-sowing. "For a wife," the letter continued, "you should choose a suitable, attractive and sweet-charactered girl before she has met anyone else she might fall for."

Already the requirement that Charles, as heir to the throne, marry someone without, as Mountbatten put it, "a past," may have undermined a relationship with a woman for whom the bachelor prince had fallen hard. Charles was just 22 when he

"The prince fell deeply in love with Camilla," his biographer Penny Juror once said. Above: the two chatted at a polo match in 1975.

"As he enters his second quarter century, he is coming into a vigorous and self-confident young manhood," *People*'s 1974 cover story declared.

1422

November 11, 1974 • 40¢

People weekly

PRINCE CHARLES

He's turning 26 without a future queen in sight

t home with Dali: 'm a better enius than painter'

ottoms brothers, an cting family eads for the top

aroline Kennedy on orseback: risking pills as Mom watches

eorge Harrison, a eatle on tour again

ickey Cohen's izarre offer to escue Patty Hearst

As smitten as Charles was with Camilla, she was not considered to be a suitable future Queen of England. Left: A polo match encounter in 1975, after her marriage.

Right: Leaving the Royal Opera House in 1975.

Camilla, the *Sunday Mirror* once wrote, "has the ability to bring the prince out of introspective moods." Below: Mrs. Parker-Bowles (in blue) appeared at another 1975 opera reception where Charles spoke with a cousin, Princess Alexandra.

met Camilla Shand, 23, a debutante and a familiar face on the polo grounds where her on-and-off boyfriend Andrew Parker Bowles played on Charles's team. "Camilla was sexy, bold and had a devil-may-care attitude. What she had was chutzpah," her biographer Christopher Wilson told *People* in 2005. In the apocryphal story of their 1971 meeting, Camilla is said to have propositioned Charles with the line: "My great-grandmother and your great-great-grandfather were lovers. So how about it?" (Alice Keppel, Camilla's great-grandmother, indeed had had a tryst with King Edward VII.) "She always liked the connection," a schoolmate told *People*.

The two began a romance, hitting the London nightclubs and spending weekends at Mountbatten's Broadlands estate. "He lost his heart to her almost at once," biographer Jonathan Dimbelby wrote. But could a woman known to have had prior relationships be a candidate for future Queen? Moreover, was Charles ready to settle down?

What happened next remains the subject of debate: Some insiders say Charles proposed in 1972, but, not wanting to compromise her privacy, Camilla turned him down, saying she "loved him but could not marry him," Mountbatten's former private secretary told *People*. Others speculate

Camilla's 1973 wedding to Andrew Parker Bowles hit the prince hard, but he remained friendly with them both.

that Charles felt pressure from family members who thought Shand an unsuitable match and used the excuse of a six-month tour with the Royal Navy to make his exit. Another theory (one viewers of *The Crown* will recognize) suggests that Mountbatten, a former admiral of the fleet, orchestrated his great-nephew's departure to keep him far from Shand, whom he once called "excellent mistress material" but little more, according to Camilla's biographer Caroline Graham.

Whatever the reason, while Charles was at sea, Camilla accepted a proposal from Andrew Parker Bowles; they married in July 1973. When Charles heard the news, he was heartbroken, writing to his uncle Dickie, "I suppose the feeling of emptiness will pass eventually." Nevertheless, he remained close with the couple, and when their son Tom was born in 1974, they made Charles the boy's godfather.

It was then that Mountbatten issued his directive to play the field, which Charles evidently took to heart. To read the press of the day, the young prince would zip about town with his dates in a blue Aston-Martin convertible and had little trouble finding company. "Tall, elegantly handsome and blue-eyed, he has an assurance and grace beyond his years," *People* wrote in 1973, calling him "the world's most eligible bachelor."

Charles saw his every flirtation chronicled in the press with the constant question: Is she the one? He largely took the guessing game in stride: "Which one of you am I going to be engaged to tomorrow?" he teased a group of women who came to greet him during a 1973 visit to Scotland. Some of his companions, however, were less amused by the attention. "[It was] pretty intolerable," ex-girlfriend Jane Ward told *People* years after their 1978 romance. Tabloid reporters "broke into my house, left notes, followed me everywhere. It was definitely a deterrent." Another, Lady Jane Welles-

ANNE & CAMILLA'S EX

BEFORE HE PROPOSED TO CAMILLA SHAND, ANDREW PARKER BOWLES DATED CHARLES'S SISTER ANNE

Just before Prince Charles first met Camilla Shand, Andrew Parker Bowles was dating Charles's sister Princess Anne for a short time in 1970. Parker Bowles, a major in the Blues and Royals regiment, was well-acquainted with the royal family, having served as a page at Queen Elizabeth's 1953 coronation. He and Anne hit it off when Parker Bowles was invited to Windsor for Royal Ascot. At the time, Anne had acquired a reputation for a lively social life that included, *Time* magazine reported, dancing till dawn at London hot spots. And "last year she sent Britons into paroxysms of one sort or another when she jumped onstage for the finale of the rock musical *Hair* and spent 10 wild minutes dancing with cast members, many of whom were scantily clad." Feisty and independent, Anne once declared, "They will have a job marrying me off to someone I don't want," but the truth was, no matter how much she liked Parker Bowles, their relationship was doomed. For one thing, because Parker Bowles was Catholic he would have been an unlikely match for the only daughter of the Queen, who is the head of the Church of England. Despite the blink-and-you-miss-it nature of their romance, the two remained very close. Anne and her first husband, Mark Phillips, chose Andrew to be one of the godfathers to their daughter Zara after she was born in 1981, and more recently the two were photographed sharing a laugh at Royal Ascot.

ley, a family friend whom Charles had invited to Sandringham in 1973 for a weekend in the country, broke it off after being hounded at the shop where she worked. In 1977 he courted Lady Sarah Spencer, whose family, including her then 16-year-old sister Diana, had grown up on the Queen's Sandringham estate. (Their father was a former equerry to the Queen.) After a Swiss Alps ski holiday, Sarah dished to a magazine in 1978 that Charles was a "romantic who falls in love easily," adding, "I'm not in love with him. And I wouldn't marry anyone I didn't love whether he were the dustman or the King of England." Naturally she was out.

Nearly 30, Charles was reaching the age at which he'd said he planned to marry. "I've fallen in love with all sorts of girls," he said in 1975 to *Woman's Own* magazine. But "falling madly in love with someone is not necessarily the starting point to getting married. Marriage is a much more important business." He told guests at a dinner in 1978, "A wife—I'm sure that's what I do need." He was still single the following summer, when, on Aug. 27, 1979, Mountbatten was killed in Ireland by an IRA bomb. Devastated, Charles leaned on old friends like Camilla Parker Bowles. Sometime later, at a friend's barbecue a young woman mentioned how sad he had appeared after Mountbatten's death. It was Sarah Spencer's sister Diana.

Before Diana caught his eye, Charles dated her older sister Sarah (far left, in 1977). The prince is a "romantic who falls in love easily," she told a British magazine in 1978.

Lady Jane Wellesley (left, in 1978) resented the media glare she was under when seeing the prince.

In the '70s Charles was seen squiring a roster of mostly blue-blooded girlfriends including Jane Ward (below left), heiress Sabrina Guinness (middle) and Caroline Longman (below right).

WHO'S THAT GIRL?

FEELING PRESSURE TO MARRY, CHARLES PROPOSES TO A FULL-OF-LIFE 19-YEAR-OLD KINDERGARTEN TEACHER WITH AN IMPECCABLE PEDIGREE—AND THE POWER TO CHARM THE WORLD

Above: Diana (in Scotland in 1974) grew up on the grounds of the Queen's Sandringham estate, playing with princes Andrew and Edward and calling the Queen Aunt Lilibet.

Right: The newly engaged couple at Balmoral in May 1981. When Charles proposed, 19-year-old Diana broke into giggles. "Yes, please," she replied.

"GREAT FUN AND BOUNCY AND FULL OF LIFE," Charles would recall of his earliest impression of Lady Diana Spencer. His then-girlfriend Sarah's kid sister was wearing, he remembered, an anorak, corduroy pants and Wellington boots the day they met at a hunting shoot at Althorp, her family home. Diana would later admit she found the not-quite-30-year-old future King "pretty amazing."

A little more than two years later, in July 1980, Diana, by then 19 years old and working as a teacher at a kindergarten, and Charles met again at a post-polo barbecue. He had long since broken up with Sarah Spencer but remembered Diana. "They just clicked," Sarah later told biographer Penny Junor. It seemed, she said, "he met Miss Right, and she met Mr. Right." And according to royal watchers, Diana also fell in love with the idea of becoming the Princess of Wales.

In many ways Diana was the blue-blooded girl next door. Born July 1, 1961, the third daughter of the Viscount Althorp—a descendant of Stuart kings and an equerry (an officer in the royal household) to King George VI and to Queen Eliza-

'I'M AMAZED THAT SHE'S BRAVE ENOUGH TO TAKE ME ON'
—**PRINCE CHARLES**

beth—Diana, who as a small child called the Queen Aunt Lilibet, grew up on the grounds of Sandringham. She and her sisters would play in her family's heated pool with the boys from the big house, Prince Andrew and Prince Edward. Her parents split when she was 6 after her mother left the family for the man who became her stepfather. Diana "used to sit on the doorstep and wait for her to come back," her younger brother once said. Sent to a finishing school in Switzerland, she was an indifferent student who preferred dance to studying.

Barely 19 when they began dating, her cheeks still girlishly plump and bangs shielding her blue eyes, Diana immediately captivated Fleet Street papers, and their photographers chased her to the London kindergarten where she worked part-time. On one occasion, the school's codirector later recalled, "she was pursued like an animal, hounded into a corner with her hands over her face."

By January 1981 even the Queen was feeling rattled. When a pack of newsmen trampled through the grounds of Sandringham looking for Diana, Her Majesty snapped: "I wish you would go away!" The media glare became so intense Prince Philip wrote a letter to his son warning him that the only honorable thing to do was propose or end the relationship. Charles later told his biographer that he "interpreted his father's attitude as an ultimatum," and on Feb. 24, 1981, the couple announced their engagement.

Above: To Diana's horror, when the press snapped a picture in 1980 at her kindergarten job, her skirt appeared transparent in the light. Seeing the papers, "she went crimson," a colleague recalled.

Above right: Diana poses with her future mother-in-law in March 1981, soon after the engagement was announced.

Right: Already a big draw, Diana greets a crowd outside Broadlands in March 1981.

Left: At a polo club 17 days before their wedding. "Prince Charles was the first man she dated," a childhood friend told *People* in 1997. "She was head over heels in love."

John Lennon
The bizarre life of his killer
Susan Ford as a mellow mom
Hazzard's ham, James Best
Designer jean ripoffs
JUNE 22, 1981 • 95c
People weekly
LADY DIANA
A sneak preview of her Big Day: the wedding gowns (all 6 of them!), the gifts, guests and the royal pain of planning it all

Above: Camilla (with Diana at a racetrack where Charles was competing in October 1980) vetted prospective princesses for Charles and gave him the okay on Diana.

"I'm amazed that she's been brave enough to take me on," Charles said in an interview that day. He had planned to give Diana time to mull over his offer, popping the question just as she was about to leave for Australia to escape the scrutiny, but Diana responded "quite promptly," she said. "It wasn't a difficult decision. It's what I want." Recalled her brother Charles years later: "She was so excited, and it was very sweet and real and lovely."

Standing stiffly before the camera in Buckingham Palace, the prince, gently stroking his young fiancée's hand, declared himself "positively delighted." Asked if they also felt "in love," Diana replied, "Of course." Charles, meanwhile, was less resolute. "Whatever 'in love' means," he said—words that might have been an early warning sign to another bride. For that day, however, his Diana saw only her happy ending. "With Prince Charles beside me, I cannot go wrong," she declared.

Only by Diana's Feb. 24, 1981, engagement, a friend would tell *People* in 1997, was it "dawning on her just what she was getting into."

PART TWO

THE FAIRY TALE

AFTER A WEDDING WATCHED BY THE WORLD, THE PRINCE AND PRINCESS OF WALES SETTLE IN TO WHAT SEEMED ON THE OUTSIDE AN IDYLLIC HOMELIFE

A day at the races! Charles and Diana (in a mohair maternity coat) enjoying the Aintree Racecourse near Liverpool for the Grand National in April 1982.

SEALED WITH A KISS

TO A GLOBAL TV AUDIENCE, THE WEDDING OF DIANA AND CHARLES LOOKED LIKE A STORYBOOK COME TO LIFE. BUT EVEN BEFORE THE BIG DAY, THE PRINCESS BRIDE HAD DOUBTS ABOUT HER GROOM'S TRUE LOVE

WATCHING THE PREWEDDING coverage on television from her bedroom as a seamstress pressed her wedding gown, the bride-to-be had a moment of panic. "Do I really have to go out in front of all these people?" Diana asked, according to seamstress Nina Missetzis. So timid as a child that she once agreed to be in a school Christmas pageant only if she didn't have to speak, Diana would soon be center stage as some 750 million watched her marry Prince Charles on July 29, 1981. Despite her nerves, she didn't disappoint when she arrived at St. Paul's Cathedral in an 1881 glass coach. In her billowing gown made of 40 yds. of silk and embroidered with 10,000 sequins and pearls, its breathtaking 25-ft. train the longest in royal history, she was princess perfection.

The newlyweds' Buckingham Palace balcony kiss, on cue from the crowd, was a first for a new royal couple in public.

"Here is the stuff of which fairy tales are made," the Archbishop of Canterbury said during the ceremony. Indeed all of London, weary from high unemployment and violent class protests at the time, seemed eager to indulge the fantasy. Buses were painted with bows, parks bloomed with Charles's royal crest outlined in blossoms, and 4,500 pots of flowers lined the wedding route, where more than half a million turned out to watch the spectacle. "We do this sort of thing rather well," Prince Charles had reflected of the pomp.

Inside the cathedral, 2,500 guests (including the groom's friend Camilla Parker Bowles—her then-husband, Andrew, commanded the Household Cavalry escort for the newlyweds) watched as Diana made the three and a half minute walk down the red-carpeted aisle on the arm of her father, the 8th Earl Spencer. Diana, on her insistence, did not promise to obey her new husband, a switch that caused a sensation at the time.

But that show of independence belied Diana's own insecurities. Days earlier she had discovered a bracelet engraved with the letters "G" and "F"—the initials of Charles and Camilla's pet names for each other, Gladys and Fred, a gift that Charles intended to give to Camilla. Diana was distraught but felt compelled to go on with the show. "We didn't want to disappoint the public," she later said. As her sisters told her, "Your face is on the tea towels, so it's too late to chicken out." During their Mediterranean honeymoon cruise, Charles sported "C&C" cuff links that Camilla had given him earlier, according to biographer Penny Junor.

The night before the wedding, however, Diana's mood improved when Charles sent her a signet ring and an affectionate card that read, "I'm so proud of you, and when you come up, I'll be there at the altar for you tomorrow. Just look 'em in the eye and knock 'em dead." And so she did. As her dress designer Elizabeth Emanuel later told *People,* "For just that day, things seemed to be right."

Camilla (above, in the pews at St. Paul's Cathedral) attended while her husband, Andrew Parker Bowles, worked security for the wedding.

The 4½-ft., 224-lb. wedding cake was locked in a room at the Royal Navy Cookery School before the nuptials. The largest layer baked for 8½ hours.

"The woman who marries me is marrying into the family business," said Charles (with the wedding party at Buckingham Palace). After the wedding the Queen and Prince Philip reportedly partied past midnight.

A tiny 18-karat gold horseshoe tucked into her dress for luck not withstanding, Diana later said, "I felt I was the lamb to the slaughter."

'I HIGHLY RECOMMEND IT. IT'S A MARVELOUS LIFE'
—DIANA ON HER NEW MARRIAGE

4
4

"I desperately loved my husband, and I wanted to share everything," Diana said in 1995. Below: a public kiss during a polo match in 1985. Right: in Canada in 1983.

COME RAIN OR SHINE

THE HONEYMOON GIVES WAY TO A NEW LIFE: ROYAL TOURS ABROAD AND, AT HOME, THE ARRIVAL OF SONS WILLIAM AND HARRY. BUT THE PICTURE ISN'T ALWAYS PERFECT FOR DIANA

THE HONEYMOONERS STRODE hand in hand through the Scottish heather, stopping on the banks of the River Dee to pose as 60 or so photographers snapped away. "I hope you're pleased with the picturesque view," Prince Charles said, gesturing toward the moors behind them. But for the press on the grounds of Balmoral for a photo session on Aug. 19, 1981, the wild beauty of the highlands was incidental; their lenses were aimed squarely at a new princess in love. "She kept putting her head on his shoulder," photographer Jayne Fincher said to *People* in 2017. "They looked so in love."

The British public was as smitten with them as the newlyweds appeared to be with each other. When the couple arrived in Wales in October 1981 for their first official appearance together, thousands turned out to see that newlywed glow in person. The crowds were so eager to touch their new princess that Diana had trouble wresting away her hand when she greeted them. But neither an overly enthusiastic reception or the blustery weather seemed to dampen the couple's spirits. "Darling, don't walk out in the rain—you'll get wet," Charles called out to Diana, taking an umbrella from her lady-in-waiting and holding it over his wife's ostrich-feather hat as the two approached fans in Carm-

People
weekly
AUGUST 16, 1982 ■ $1.00
Sinatra, R.J. Wagne
Jill St. John and Carso
open an L.A. showplac
Facts of Life in Pari
Broadway's X-rated sta
KING OF HEARTS
A royal christening—
and a touching
moment for Diana
and her little prince
0 10227
33
724414

Above: In their first years together, the couple (in Gibraltar during their August 1981 honeymoon) did have "interludes of happiness," as Charles's biographer later put it.

Left: At his christening Aug. 4, 1982, William was kept content during his photo shoot by sucking on his mother's pinkie.

arthen. "I am oblivious to the weather," she said, continuing on through the showers. "It's the warmth of the welcome that matters." After a lifetime in the spotlight, the prince seemed pleased to finally have someone to share the stage. When crowds betrayed some disappointment at shaking his hand while Diana was elsewhere, he told them with a good-natured shrug, "I'm afraid there is only one Princess of Wales."

It wasn't long before another new star was on the scene. Prince William Arthur Philip Louis was born June 21, 1982, 328 days after the royal wedding. As a boy, he was of course heir to the throne, but more important to his parents, he'd captured their hearts. Greeting well-wishers two hours after the birth, Charles called the experience "rather a shock to my system" but that he was "relieved and delighted," and he declared his new son "in marvelous form." Before his arrival, the couple made it clear that theirs would be a new kind of royal family. Breaking with tradition, Diana chose to deliver at London's St. Mary's Hospital rather than at Buckingham Palace, and Charles insisted on being at his wife's side during her six hours of labor (his father, Prince Philip, was famously playing racquetball when Charles arrived). "I am, after all, the father, and I suppose I started this whole business," Prince Charles had said. "So I intend to be there when everything happens."

They continued their hands-on parenting as William grew, taking turns giving him his bath and telling him bedtime stories. The new father "can't stop talking about the baby," one British paper wrote at the time. And when the couple were

Above: The couple thrilled donors as they danced to "Isn't She Lovely" at a charity dinner in Melbourne in 1985. Right: playing with William in 1984 at Kensington Palace.

'SHE WAS SO THRILLED. DIANA ALWAYS WANTED TO HAVE A FAMILY'
—DIANA'S BROTHER CHARLES SPENCER

sent on a six-week tour to New Zealand and Australia in May 1983, Diana again broke precedent, persuading a reluctant Queen to allow their 10-month-old son to join. The tot thrilled reporters with a 15-minute crawl-about on a rug spread outside Auckland's Government House. "The very fact that he sees so much of his mother and father—and that they refuse to be separated from him unless it is really necessary—is different from what even Prince Charles experienced," Diana's father said.

On Sept. 15, 1984, after a second difficult pregnancy ("I'm not made for the production line," Diana ruefully joked), Prince Henry Charles Albert David was born, giving Wills a brother and the country a spare to the heir. Charles declared himself thrilled—"It didn't matter whether it was a boy or a girl"—and revealed big brother's excitement. "William has taken to the new baby like a duck to water," Charles confided at the time to one of his groundsmen, according to *People*. "It's worth a guinea a minute watching him enjoy himself. He's been climbing in and out of Harry's cot." But Diana was feeling the mounting pressure of her position. "One minute I was a nobody, the next minute I was Princess of Wales, mother, media toy, member of this family, and it was just too much for one person to handle," she later said. All eyes were on her, often to her dismay—and sometimes to her husband's.

Left: A getaway to an Austrian ski resort turned into a debacle when Diana refused to pose for pictures. "She's behaving like a spoiled brat," the *Daily Mail's* acid-penned columnist Nigel Dempster complained. Above: Diana and Charles leave St. Mary's Hospital on Sept. 16, 1984, the day after Prince Harry was born. Below: the royal family aboard the Royal Yacht *Britannia* in Venice in April 1985.

William and Harry grew up near five cousins who lived at Kensington Palace. Playtime at Windsor Castle included "crawl on the floor" play with Granny.

THE PEOPLE'S PRINCESS

CHARLES TAUGHT 'SHY DI' HOW TO MEET THE PUBLIC. A QUICK STUDY, SHE SOON SCHOOLED THE PRINCE IN THE ART OF CHARMING THEM

Above: The Prince and Princess of Wales arrive in Auckland, New Zealand, on April 17, 1983. Left: In 1985, *People* estimated Diana's value to the British nation—in tourism, fashion and publicity for the U.K.—at $500 million.

IN MARCH 1983 CHARLES, DIANA and their 9-month old son William set off on a six-week tour of Australia and New Zealand in what was then a break with tradition. Customarily royal children would stay behind with nannies when their parents traveled abroad. But the new mum would have none of it. Mindful of the painful separations that Charles had experienced in his youth when his parents were away, Diana insisted on taking Wills, and the trip was a success, both publicly and for the young family. The couple "were extremely happy" there, Charles wrote to a friend. "The great joy was that we were entirely alone together."

The joy of the marriage, however, did not last. Bound by devotion to duty, the couple, who otherwise had few interests in common, initially worked well together in public. Throngs of fans and reporters showed up for their engagements. The attraction, however, wasn't shared equally. Describing the couple's first official trip, to Wales in 1981, Sally Bedell Smith writes in

Prince Charles: The Passions and Paradoxes of an Improbable Life that crowds chanted "We want Diana!," prompting Charles good-naturedly to commiserate with the people he greeted, saying, "You'll have to make do with me." Interviewed by *People* in a pub in Caernarvon, Wales, one admirer explained, "She has the common touch that people love." By the time of the 1983 tour, when Diana-mania seemed to grip Australia and New Zealand, the popularity gap had grown painfully wide. Looking back years later at the rapturous reception she met there while her husband was all but ignored, Diana admitted to the BBC's Martin Bashir that the spouses were becoming more like rivals. "When we flew back from New Zealand, I was a different person," she said. "I realized the sense of duty, the level of intensity of interest and the demanding role I now found myself in." It was "either sink or swim," she said.

Diana—who began most mornings with laps in the Buckingham Palace pool—determined to swim. Her calendar grew to 250 events a year in the mid-1980s. (In 1984 she and Charles each made solo appearances in the county of Hampshire; her turnout reportedly dwarfed his 10 to 1.) An editor at *British Vogue* helped to shape her wardrobe. She became a polished public speaker. And a spin on the dance floor with John Travolta at a 1985 White House dinner (a pairing orchestrated by hostess Nancy Reagan) proclaimed Diana's Hollywood-level celebrity on both sides of the Atlantic. Yet back at home some of her husband's friends and staff were decidedly less entranced. Since the couple's marriage four years earlier, 40-odd employees had either left or been dismissed—an astonishing number for a royal residence, where staffers frequently serve for life. One told *People* that Diana had turned the family's homes into "a minefield." Said another: "No one is in any doubt who the real ruler is in Charles and Diana's household. Below stairs, everyone calls her the Boss."

Top: At a White House gala during Charles and Diana's 1985 visit to Washington, the princess danced with John Travolta to a medley of songs from *Saturday Night Fever* and *Grease*. "She was the most beautiful woman in the room," Travolta told *People*. Right: Diana competed with other parents at Prince William's school's sports day in 1989. Far right: An estimated 1 million well-wishers turned out to greet the royal couple during their 1983 trip to Australia.

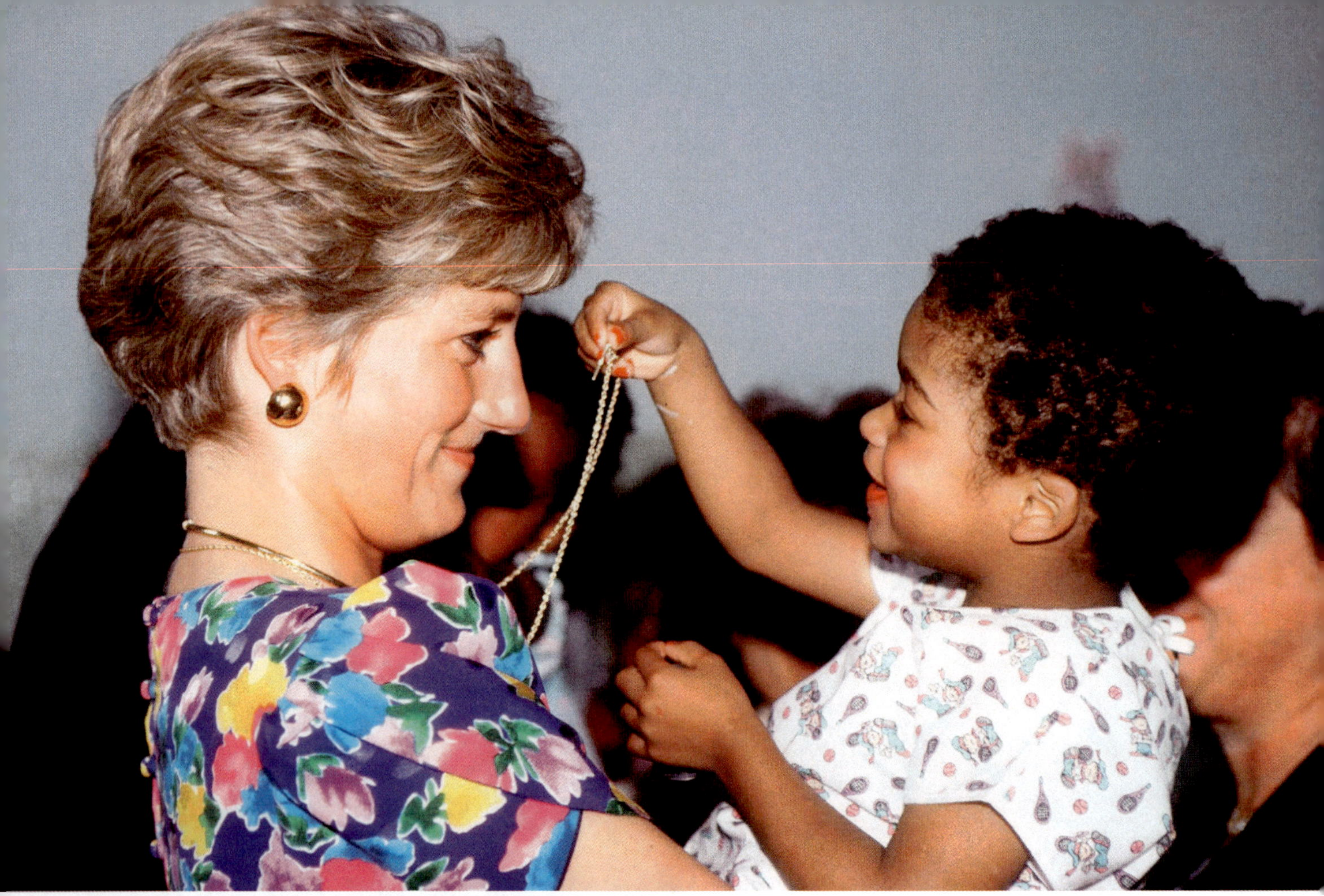

Above: A former kindergarten teaching assistant and nanny, Diana (with a resident of a shelter for abandoned children with HIV/AIDS in São Paulo) made frequent public displays of compassion. Left: In 1991 the musical princess played the piano for patients at a children's hospital in Prague.

Overshadowed by the increasingly confident Princess of Wales and frustrated that the public showed more interest in her clothes than in causes he held important, such as the environment or his quixotic crusade against modern architecture, Charles cut back his engagements. "He can no longer see rhyme or reason in continuing the tireless rounds of ceremonial appearances and handshaking. He doesn't know what to do with himself," observed *Daily Mail* royal watcher Nigel Dempster.

Shortly after, Diana began telling friends that she would chart an independent course to the hearts of the British people. "More and more, from now on, it will seem as if we are going our separate ways—and we will be," she said 1987. "When we were first married, I needed Charles at my side to help me learn the ropes, which were almost completely unknown to me. Now I can cope on my own."

Diana, stunning in a gown by favorite designer Bruce Oldfield in 1989, was recognized as a boon to the British fashion industry.

Princess Diana and Prince Charles looking quite glum on a royal tour of Canada, Oct. 25, 1991.

PART THREE

THEIR TROUBLES

AFTER SUSPICIONS (AND ADMISSIONS) OF CHEATING, CAN THIS MARRIAGE BE SAVED? THE ESTRANGED COUPLE CARRY ON FOR YEARS BEFORE THE QUEEN CALLS THE WHOLE THING OFF

People
OCTOBER 31, 1988 ■ $1.69
weekly
Reaching 40,
CHARLES
builds a private
LIFE WITHOUT
DI
While he fishes,
paints, broods
over the symbols
in his dreams &
dallies abroad,
Diana gets
a taste
of single
motherhood
44
10227
0 724414 8

MORE THAN OLD FRIENDS

BY 1986 CHARLES AND CAMILLA WERE SECRETLY LOVERS AGAIN. WHILE DIANA, IN THE KNOW, ALSO FOUND COMFORT OUTSIDE THE MARRIAGE

SITUATED IN THE HEART OF THE BUCOLIC Cotswolds region, Charles's Highgrove estate has served as a rural retreat since he purchased the Georgian mansion in 1980. Gardening, hunting and playing polo nearby keep him happy in the country. The prince's 340-acre spread is also conveniently close to the country homes of his sister Anne and several of the old aristocratic friends who make up the so-called Highgrove Set, among them British Army officer Andrew Parker Bowles and his family, who lived at Middlewick House, 11 miles away.

As tensions deepened between the essentially incompatible Prince and Princess of Wales, old pals Charles and Camilla Parker Bowles began spending more time together. Both were members of Britain's premier fox-and-hounds club, the Duke of Beaufort's Hunt. Sequestered behind stone walls and hedges, Highgrove became the perfect place for their romantic reconciliation.

By 1986 Charles and Diana's residences were houses divided. Diana began to avoid Highgrove, where Charles's friends collected on the weekend, and spent

Above: Their affair still secret, Prince Charles and Camilla Parker Bowles were surprised by a photographer on a trip to Turkey in 1989.

Left: "One thing is horribly clear: The Waleses have almost nothing in common except their children—and their inability to communicate," *People* noted in 1988.

Left: Diana hinted that she fell "deeply in love" with bodyguard Barry Mannakee (together in 1985) in comments published after her death.

Right: As her son William looked on, Diana presented a riding trophy to ex-Life Guards Maj. James Hewitt at the height of their affair in 1989.

Below: The royal couple couldn't hide the strain of being together during their 1992 trip to South Korea, their last official joint engagement.

more time with her own crew, dining out and shopping in London. On evenings when Diana was away, servants at the family's Gloucestershire estate began to note the sound of Charles's Aston Martin sports car repeatedly scrunching across the gravel drive after dinner and his return well into the night. As he would later admit, his destination was Middlewick, where he and Camilla enjoyed trysts while her husband was working near London.

Rumors of the prince's nighttime visits reached Diana, who reportedly confirmed them by pressing the "last number dialed" key on Charles's mobile phone. But Diana had her own secrets to keep. Frustrated and lonely in her marriage, the princess turned for comfort to a string of the personal security officers assigned to protect her, including one, Barry Mannakee, with whom palace insiders suspected she had fallen in love. She was devastated when Mannakee, a fatherly figure, was abruptly transferred to other duties in the summer of 1986—she blamed her husband or officials loyal to him for the move—and was deeply depressed when the former aide was killed in a motorcycle crash the following year.

Diana wasn't alone for long. Her relationship with handsome cavalry officer James Hewitt began after he was hired to give her riding lessons earlier that year. Hewitt, who later betrayed Diana by writing tell-all books and reportedly offered to sell dozens of letters and cards she had written to him during their five-year affair, claimed that Diana made the first move—a kiss one day at the officers' mess at Windsor Castle. She invited him to Highgrove, where, he says, he gamely participated in pillow fights and read William and Harry bedtime stories.

If Charles—who, Hewitt said, had "tacit knowledge" of his relationship with Diana—was at home with Camilla, Diana often joined Hewitt at his mother's modest Devon farmhouse. In his memoir *A Royal Duty,* Paul Burrell, Diana's fiercely loyal butler, recalled his boss sending him to pick up a friend at a railway station near Highgrove. When Burrell returned with Hewitt, Diana embraced her guest like a lover. "She was glowing," he wrote.

In many ways Prince Charles's on-again lover was anything but the stereotypical other woman. At 38, Camilla was a married mother of two grown children who was happiest "hunting for grouse in a howling wind," as one friend told *People.* Partial to jodhpurs and Wellington boots, she had none of Diana's glamour or uncanny PR savvy. When the Princess of Wales had visited the HIV ward of a London hospital in 1987, it prompted veteran royals reporter Judy Wade to say, "Shaking hands with an AIDS patient is the most important thing a royal's done in 200 years."

In Camilla's familiar warmth and earthy humor, Charles had found the love of his life. But if he thought he and Diana, having provided an heir and a spare to the nation, could settle into a new, laissez-faire phase of their marriage, he was seriously mistaken. Diana fumed at her husband's infidelity and had no intention of stepping aside. At a 40th-birthday party for Camilla's sister Annabel in London in 1989, Diana sat down for a private chat with her husband's mistress. "I'm sorry I'm in the way, I obviously am in the way, and it must be hell for both of you," she would later say she told Camilla. "But I do know what is going on. Don't treat me like an idiot."

AIRING THEIR LAUNDRY IN PUBLIC

THE TRUTH—OR VERSIONS OF IT—COMES OUT IN HIS AND HERS CONFESSIONAL INTERVIEWS, PROMPTING THE QUEEN TO CALL FOR THE COUPLE TO DIVORCE

In Diana's 1995 interview with the BBC's Martin Bashir (top left and above) she said her husband's affair with Camilla Parker Bowles (top right, on the cover of *People*) destroyed their marriage and was a factor in her developing "rampant bulimia."

IN MAY 1991 AN UNASSUMING MAN ON A BICYCLE pulled up to the wrought-iron gates of Kensington Palace and asked to see Princess Diana. Dr. James Colthurst, a trusted friend from Diana's single days, spent hours that day—and on five other occasions over the course of the summer and into autumn—talking to the princess about her life and her marriage. Acting as a secret go-between, he then handed off the tape recordings of the intimate interviews to author Andrew Morton, whose biography *Diana: Her True Story* exploded like a grenade lobbed from behind the palace gates when it was published the following year. "Diana Driven to Five Suicide Attempts by 'Uncaring' Charles" declared the headline in the respected *Sunday Times* on June 7, 1992.

Morton's book, which became a global bestseller, marked a new phase in the acrimonious misalliance of the Prince and Princess of Wales, which would henceforth be fought out in the press. It revealed the eating disorder that had plagued Diana since her engagement to Charles; her struggle to fit in with Charles and what she saw as his unfeeling family; and her desperate plea for help by throwing herself down a staircase while pregnant with William and cutting her arms and legs with a knife. The book targeted Camilla Parker Bowles as the culprit in the collapse of the Waleses' marriage—"the rottweiler," Diana called her—and described the day happiness turned to grief when the couple's son Harry was born in 1984. Charles couldn't disguise his disappointment that the child wasn't the daughter he had longed for and dismissively noted his red hair, a common Spencer trait. That day a crushed Diana told friends, "Something inside me died." It was the beginning of the end, she said.

While Buckingham Palace strenuously denied that Diana had cooperated with her biographer—although, in fact, she had—the book was undoubtedly a reliable portrait of her private pain. Citing a letter Diana wrote to her father, Morton quotes her as saying about the book, "It is a chance for my own self to surface a little, rather than be lost in the system. I rather see it as a lifebelt against being drowned."

Public sympathy was largely on Diana's side, at least initially. Newspaper columnists speculated that Charles was unsuited for marriage—and the throne. The Archbishop of Canterbury expressed his concern about the book's effects on the couple's children. When at her next official engagement the

Above: The tabloids dubbed the couple the Glums during their 1992 trip to South Korea. They split the following month.

Above right: Diana wore a daring off-the-rack design by Christina Stambolian to a London fundraiser the night that her husband admitted to adultery on TV. Her "Revenge Dress" later fetched $74,000 at a charity auction, about 40 times the original price.

Right: Journalist Jonathan Dimbleby (with Charles at Highgrove for his confessional interview on June 15, 1994) wrote a 620-page biography of the prince widely seen as an attempt to rehabilitate his image.

Murphy Brown's real nemesis: her boss, Miles

SEPTEMBER 14, 1992 $1.99

People weekly

Candice Bergen & Grant Shau

DIANA'S SECRETS

The furor over the tape, the tattletale, and two men too close to Di

Below: Diana's intimate friend James Gilbey; at left, her riding instructo Major James Hewitt

0 724414 8
10227
3

'EVERYTHING CHANGED AFTER WE SEPARATED, AND LIFE BECAME VERY DIFFICULT THEN FOR ME... I WAS THE SEPARATED WIFE OF THE PRINCE OF WALES; I WAS A PROBLEM, FULL STOP'

—DIANA TO THE BBC, 1995

vulnerable princess began to tear up, the chairman of a Merseyside cancer hospice offered words of support.

Camilla, however, was unflappable. On the day that excerpts of the Morton book debuted, she and her husband, Andrew, turned up to watch a polo game at Windsor Great Park. In a move symbolic of the Queen's support, the couple were seated in the royal enclosure and invited to tea. Afterward, Camilla told reporters, "I'm certainly not going to bury myself away because of what the papers say. Absolutely not. Why should I?"

Later that summer transcripts of an intimate chat between Diana and one of her oldest friends, James Gilbey, an heir to the gin fortune, surfaced in *The Sun*. Allegedly captured by a pair of ham radio operators, the pirated conversation included Diana complaining that she felt "sad and empty" and that her husband made life "real torture." Dubbed Squidgygate, after the pet name Gilbey used 53 times on the tapes, the ensuing scandal was heightened days later by the revelations of a former Army corporal who claimed that, in 1988, he had seen the princess embrace her riding instructor James Hewitt. Diana, it was now obvious, was not an entirely blameless victim.

Nor was she inclined to back down from headlines that she believed were orchestrated by her husband's "men in gray." After Britain's prime minister John Major announced that Charles and Diana had agreed to separate in late 1992, it was Charles's turn to squirm. A London tabloid published excerpts from another clandestinely recorded phone call, this time a raunchy bedtime

Diana (left, on *People* in 1992) admitted her affair with James Hewitt but denied that the man on the leaked "Squidgygate" tapes, James Gilbey (top right), was her lover. Another admirer, married London art dealer Oliver Hoare (right), reportedly visited Diana at Kensington Palace by hiding in the trunk of a car.

conversation between Charles and Camilla as they planned their next assignation:

Camilla: Mmm. You're awfully good at feeling your way along.

Charles: Oh, stop! I want to feel my way along you, all over you…

The so-called Camillagate tapes—which Diana labeled "sick"—proved what most people in Britain already knew: The heir to the throne was having an affair with a married woman. However, Diana—who surprised Buckingham Palace by announcing that she would drastically scale back her role in public life, devoting herself to just six of the 100 or so royal patronages that had previously filled her calendar—remained, in a twist on her acronym POW, the Prisoner of Wales. Charles reportedly told the Queen that any hope of marital reconciliation had now passed, while Diana, the child of divorced parents who said she feared the impact of a split on her sons, continued to cling to the prestige of being the wife of the future King. As part of the publicity campaign mapped out by his beefed-up press office, Charles cooperated with BBC journalist Jonathan Dimbleby, who wrote a serious-minded biography detailing the prince's wide-ranging interests and diplomatic endeavours, and taped an TV interview in which Charles fessed up to his love for Camilla, now the unofficial hostess of Highgrove.

Not to be upstaged, on the night the BBC aired the interview, Diana arrived at the opening of an exhibit at London's Serpentine Gallery swathed in a sexy black chiffon minidress that instantly gained notoriety as the Revenge Dress. It was her own tell-all interview on BBC's *Panorama*, however, that finally put the iron stake in the wheezing heart of the Waleses' marriage. Before a global TV audience estimated at 21 million viewers, Diana sadly recounted that "there were three of us in this marriage, so it was a bit crowded." Asked if she believed she would still be queen one day, she told TV journalist Martin Bashir, "I'd like to be queen of people's hearts."

Dismayed by the couple's corrosive game of one-upmanship, the Queen officially urged the couple to legally call it quits for the sake of the children and the nation. It took months for the parties to negotiate the terms: Diana received $600,000 per year, her apartment in Kensington Palace and a $27 million settlement. As a former member of the royal family, she was henceforth to be known as Diana, Princess of Wales, but no longer addressed as "Your Royal Highness." The fairy tale had ended years before. The tawdry soap opera was now over as well.

Far left: On the 40th anniversary of her succession, the Queen called 1992—when both Charles and Diana and Andrew and Fergie legally separated—an annus horribilis, a horrible year.

After Charles and Diana (left, in 1988) admitted that their marriage was irretrievably broken, Buckingham Palace issued an unprecedented statement in 1995 calling for them to divorce.

XMAS EXCLUSIVE

FREE TAKE THAT POSTER

25p

READ HIM TODAY ON PAGE EIGHT

QUEEN TELLS DI TO SPLIT

1,000 knives AMAZING START TO AMNESTY

Daily Express

GENE BREAKTHROUGH IN BATTLE AGAINST BREAST CANCER

JUDGE BACKS RIGHT TO HIT A THUG

Queen orders Diana divorce

Daily Mail

Could you survive 19 parties in one week?

Charles agrees to marriage split but Diana

QUEEN ORD

ROYAL DIVO

THE Sun 25p

The Sun's the paper.. TODAY ...for Today readers

Sun World Exclusive

QUEEN ORDERS

THE TI

Queen urges Prince t

Letter expresses frustration over

OnLine

The world's most famous journalist

PART FOUR
AFTER THE SPLIT

CHARLES'S AND DIANA'S NEW LIVES LOOK VERY DIFFERENT. SHE'S A PHILANTHROPIST AND FASHION ICON DATING ACROSS BORDERS. HE BEGINS TO THINK OF MAKING A CLANDESTINE LOVE LEGITIMATE TO THE PUBLIC. BUT A YEAR AFTER THE DIVORCE, TRAGEDY STRIKES

In 1996 Diana visited Pakistan, reportedly to discuss moving there in order to marry her lover Hasnat Khan. Opposite: Back at home, single dad Charles met the Spice Girls at a Royal Opera House gala in 1997.

MAKING HER OWN PATH

HAVING LEFT BEHIND ROYAL DUTIES, DIANA DEVOTED HERSELF TO HER BOYS AND TO CAUSES SHE CARED ABOUT. SHE TRAVELED WIDELY, FELL IN LOVE AND FOLLOWED WHERE HER HEART LED HER

HER LONG nightmare was over. Single again at 35 and filled with optimism, Diana, no longer royal but still a princess to her people, met with Britain's prime minister, Tony Blair, to discuss her new role as a humanitarian emissary. In an act that seemed to turn the page on the past and signal a new future free of the courtly flummery she had grown to despise, she auctioned off 79 dresses from her

Right: In 1997 Diana made headlines when she walked through a cleared area in a live minefield that had been laid during Angola's civil war. Below: Still Mum, she took William to the dentist in London.

BRITISH
RED CROSS
THE
HALO
TRUST

[DIANA] MUST HAVE A ROLE IN PUBLIC LIFE, AND AS I SEE IT, ALWAYS WILL"
—JOHN MAJOR, THEN U.K. PRIME MINISTER

years as a prince's wife at Christie's for charity. "Nothing gives me more happiness," Diana told *Le Monde* in 1997, "than to try to aid the most vulnerable in this society."

Diana saw more of her acquaintances, including Hayat Palumbo, a British socialite, and Lucia Flecha de Lima, wife of the Brazilian ambassador to the U.S., at whose summer home on Martha's Vineyard she occasionally stayed, far from Fleet Street and the Establishment in London. She visited her little brother Charles, the Ninth Earl Spencer, in South Africa and triggered a frenzy in New York City when she bypassed a discreet VIP entrance to walk up the stairs of the Metropolitan Museum of Art for a gala to benefit its Costume Institute in 1996.

The princess told a friend, Palm Beach accessories designer Lana Marks, that "she was looking forward to getting married again, and she wanted to have a little girl." There were suitors, to be sure. She became friendly with Dr. Hasnat Khan, a London cardiologist, and reportedly went so far as to travel to Pakistan to meet his family before he broke off the relationship because of the ever-present press in 1997.

By July she had met Dodi Al Fayed, 42, an Egyptian-born movie producer (an Oscar winner for *Chariots of Fire*) whose father was the multimillionaire owner of Harrods and other British heritage brands. Their whirlwind romance began when the older Al Fayed, who had been friendly with her father, Johnnie Spencer, the Eighth Earl Spencer, invited Diana and her boys to join his family at his Saint-Tropez villa. Soon Diana and Dodi were vacationing on their own, aboard the family's yacht and in Paris, where the Al Fayeds own the Hotel Ritz.

Dodi was by anybody's measure a spoiled playboy, but he offered Diana comfort, a

Above: Prince William's confirmation at Windsor Castle on March 9, 1997, was the last time the family was photographed together. The Queen sat beside Charles, and William's godparents stood behind them.

Left: It was Prince William's idea to sell Diana's gowns for charity. Here, the princess at a pre-auction event at Christie's in New York City on June 23, 1997.

Right: "He has given me all the things I need," Diana told a friend of Pakistani-born heart surgeon Hasnat Khan (in January 1997), whom she met while visiting a patient at a London hospital in 1995.

sense of humor and security. Even so, on one of the trips to the South of France, Diana steered a speedboat toward a boat of floating photographers and, after appealing for privacy, taunted them mercilessly. "You're going to be surprised with the next thing I do." Two weeks later, after paparazzi pursued Diana and her love at high speed through the streets of Paris, she and Dodi, along with the driver Henri Paul, died in a car crash. Her second act ended before it barely began.

"She can relax. Why shouldn't she? She's single, he's single. They like each other," said the *Daily Mail*'s Richard Kay of Diana and her new guy, Dodi Al Fayed (left, together in Saint-Tropez in 1997, and, right, on the cover of *People*).

Below: During a 1996 visit to Chicago, Diana toured the Cook County Hospital pediatric ward and met with patients.

OUT OF THE SHADOWS, BRIEFLY

THEIR LOVE NO LONGER FORBIDDEN, CAMILLA AND CHARLES QUIETLY BEGIN DATING IN THE OPEN. THEY SOON RETREAT FROM VIEW, HOWEVER, WHEN THE PUBLIC IS CONSUMED WITH GRIEF FOR PRINCESS DIANA

AS DIANA HOPSCOTCHED THE WORLD in her role as philanthropist, Charles was home laying the groundwork for a formal introduction: between the British public—still smitten with his ex—and his longtime mistress turned girlfriend, Camilla Parker Bowles. "They will no longer resort to cloak-and-dagger meetings—they will come out into the open," one friend predicted to *People* at the time.

There would be obstacles, of course. Although Charles was not legally barred from divorcing or from marrying a divorcée, the future King thought his subjects would be loath to accept Camilla as their Queen. And at the time, the Church of England forbade a divorced person from remarrying in the church. Charles's attempts to claim both the crown and Camilla, said one Palace expert, "would divide the country like nothing since the abdication [of Edward VIII]. Such a division would be enough to force Charles to [give up the

Camilla arriving at the 50th-birthday party that Charles threw for her at his Highgrove estate in July 1997. His message with the event, said one observer, "was loud and clear."

In June 1997 Charles went solo to a party near Trondheim for Norway's King Harald and Queen Sonja.

In July 1996 Charles shared a light moment with the Sultan of Brunei, Hassanal Bolkiah in Bandar Seri Begawan, the capital city.

throne], just as Edward did." But in the summer of 1997, with the divorce not quite a year behind him, Charles wasn't thinking about a second wedding. Now, nearly three decades after he and Camilla had first met, he was going to celebrate her 50th birthday with a luxe party at Highgrove. On July 18 guests and press photographers saw Mrs. Parker Bowles arrive at the Gloucestershire estate in a chauffeured car. But instead of cowering from the cameras, she beamed. With this party, at which champagne flowed early into the following morning, the divorcé prince sent the public, including critics, a message. "He's saying, 'Camilla is a very important person in my life, and this is a public endorsement of our relationship,'" Peter Archer, a British Press Association royals correspondent told *People.*

Already he had begun to find a suitable public role for the woman he loved. In April of that year Camilla had become a patron of Britain's National Osteoporosis Society, and on July 6 the BBC aired a sympathetic Camilla documentary made with apparent cooperation from some of her friends. The next day London's *Daily Mail* wrote of Camilla, "Isn't it time we stopped hating this dignified woman?"

The campaign worked and the tide of public opinion seemed to start turning in his favor, with some feeling that Charles should have the chance to marry the woman he should have married in the first place.

Then, on the night of Aug. 31, 1997, in Paris, Diana and the new man in her life, Egyptian-born businessman Dodi Al Fayed, were killed in a car crash while trying to evade paparazzi. (It was later found that the driver of the Mercedes, which hit a concrete support column in a tunnel adjacent to the Seine, had a blood alcohol level three times the French legal limit.) Six days later a stunned world looked

Will and Harry spent part of summer 1997 in the Scottish Highlands while visiting Dad at Balmoral. They were there when they learned of Diana's death.

on as a genuinely grieving Charles—wearing a blue suit that Diana had picked out for him that was her favorite—and his two now-motherless sons walked behind Diana's funeral cortege. For weeks tributes to Diana poured in from around the world. Flowers that mourning fans brought to Kensington and Buckingham Palaces grew to cover acres. Elton John's song "Candle in the Wind 1997," a loving reworking of his and Bernie Taupin's 1973 hit with the money going to Diana's favorite charities, went straight to No. 1. William and Harry were kept out of view following the funeral, and Charles tended to his sons. "He was there for us," Harry said in a 2017 BBC documentary. "He was the one out of two left, and he tried to do his best and to make sure that we were protected and looked after."

"He tried to do his best and to make sure that we were protected," Harry later said of his father (viewing tributes to Diana outside Kensington Palace, 1997). "But he was going through the same grieving process."

Camilla, said to be "devastated" by Diana's death, also withdrew. "Having been the most vilified person in the country, Camilla had just about crawled out of her bunker," said her biographer Christopher Wilson. With Diana's death, Camilla would keep an exceedingly low profile for the better part of the next year. Diana's death was "bad news for Camilla," noted Ingrid Seward, editor in chief of *Majesty* magazine. "All the love that had been directed toward Diana could easily be directed in hatred toward her." Until things calmed down, it wasn't worth the risk if she and Charles were ever to have a legitimate chance of being true to their hearts. "The specter of Diana is going to haunt [Charles] until the day he dies," declared author Brian Hoey at the time. "We've seen the end to any possibility of a marriage in the near future."

PART FIVE

MEET THE DUCHESS

WITH THE FAMILY'S BLESSING, CAMILLA WEDS THE PRINCE OF WALES BUT—FOREGOING THE PRINCESS TITLE STILL LINKED TO DIANA—BECOMES 'DUCHESS OF CORNWALL' AND REVELS IN HER NEW ROYAL ROLE

Camilla in the Greville Tiara at the State Opening of Parliament in May 2016.

HAPPY AT LAST!

NEARLY THREE DECADES AFTER THEY FIRST DATED—AND AFTER YEARS OF CLANDESTINE TRYSTS—CAMILLA AND CHARLES MAKE THEIR PUBLIC DEBUT AND, DEFYING CYNICS, EVENTUALLY MARRY

THE FIRST STEP WAS JUST TEA. On June 12, 1998, nearly a year after Diana's death, Charles introduced his older son, William, then 16, to Camilla over tea at the family's St. James's Palace apartment. Though it later was billed in the press as a chance encounter, the meeting, in fact, had been orchestrated at Will's suggestion. Harry, then 13, would meet Camilla at Highgrove a few weeks later. Those initial introductions went well enough that, when the boys hosted a July 31 prebirthday celebration at Highgrove for their father—with a play written by British comic Stephen Fry and starring Emma Thompson—Camilla sat in the place of honor, next to Charles. Harry and William "don't see her as a villain," palace chronicler Judy Wade told *People* in 1998, adding that they understood that "she too has had a rough time." By the following August, Parker Bowles was so thoroughly integrated into Charles's life that she and her two children, son Tom, then 24, and daughter Laura, 21, were invited to the annual Mediterranean cruise that Charles took with William and Harry. (Charles, who is Tom's godfather, had met both Parker Bowles's kids over the years.)

Above: On Jan. 28, 1999, the press staked out the Ritz in London to capture a first picture of Charles and Camilla as a public couple.

Left: By November 1999 they were clearly comfortable being spotted leaving London's Albery Theatre after a performance of Ronald Harwood's *Quartet*, about aging opera singers.

Waterboy's Adam Sandler: Revenge of the Class Cutup!

NOVEMBER 30, 1998

People weekly

Charles at 50

NEW AND IMPROVED!

With his popularity on the rise, a recharged Charles becomes King for a Day at a raucous birthday bash with Camilla and the boys. (P.S. The Queen stayed away)

Harry and Wills toast Dad

Camilla goes glam for the party

www.people.com

In January 1999 Charles's press team spread the word that he and Camilla would be at London's Ritz Hotel attending a party for Camilla's sister. The expected crush of more than 200 paparazzi delivered the first pictures of their public debut as a couple. The BBC reported that "there were screams and whoops as Charles and Camilla walked down the steps of the Ritz toward their waiting car. One woman clapped and shouted, 'Good on you, Charlie!'"

But Charles's mother, Queen Elizabeth, did not receive his new girlfriend in such stride. "She sees Camilla as a problem she would rather not deal with," said British Press Association reporter Peter Archer. Camilla had been left off the invite list for the June 19, 1999, wedding of Prince Edward and Sophie Rhys-Jones, though that may have been custom with regard to unmarried partners, rather than a personal slight. But both the Queen and her subjects eventually softened. Another year later, in summer 2000, the Queen attended a Highgrove party with Camilla in attendance. "Marry Her!" screamed the headline in *The Daily*

Top: The Nov. 30, 1998, *People* cover story on Charles quoted a source saying, "I think he's going to have to say, 'I'm going to be King, and I intend to marry Camilla,' whether it meets the requirements of the Church of England or not."

Right: At the 2003 Sandringham Flower Show, held at the Queen's estate, Camilla had a big fan in Dorothy Edwards, 77, of Haughley.

Far right: The pair were radiant at a June 2000 gala dinner for the Prince's Trust, which supports education and community-building programs across the U.K.

Mirror two days later; a poll taken by the paper showed that 68 percent of Britons thought Charles and Camilla should tie the knot. But two more years passed before the Queen finally included Camilla at an official family function—a pop concert in honor of her Golden Jubilee, broadcast to millions from the gardens at Buckingham Palace. Fans who tuned in for headliners like Paul McCartney, Queen, Eric Clapton and Elton John might not have noticed that in the royal family's balcony, Camilla sat not far behind the Queen (though not next to Charles). "There has been a patching up and a mending of relationships," said Christopher Wilson, author of a Camilla biography, *The Windsor Knot,* to *People.* "This has all been done for the sake of family unity. And I think Charles has won the day."

The couple became engaged in February 2005. Charles gave his bride-to-be an art deco ring dating to his mother's 1926 birth. On April 9, 2005, Charles and Camilla were wed in a simple half-hour civil ceremony at Windsor Guildhall, Berkshire, followed by a

Big day: Guests at Charles and Camilla's April 2005 wedding included his sons Will and Harry, her son Tom and daughter Laura, the Queen and Prince Philip and Camilla's father, Bruce Shand.

religious service of blessing and tea-and-finger-foods reception at Windsor Castle. Guests included comedian Joan Rivers, musician Phil Collins and then-prime minister Tony Blair. When Parker Bowles arrived for the ceremony, "it was clear the crowd was on her side," said one observer. In fact, everyone was. William and Harry were beaming all day and playfully decorated the Bentley that took the newlyweds into their married life with "C+C" and "Just Married" graffiti. "The two boys were in fantastic form," Gerald Ward, Harry's godfather, told *People*. "They were both very happy." The Queen had come around, comparing Charles and Camilla's arduous journey to wedded bliss to a horse race in a toast that ended with:"My son is home and dry with the woman he loves. Welcome to the winners' enclosure." "I really do think that Charles has ended up with his soulmate," mused one wedding guest. The couple's friend Patti Palmer-Tomkinson agreed in *The New Yorker*: "After all this time, they are just happy to breathe the same air."

CHARLES AND CAMILLA TODAY

OFFICIAL DUTIES FILL THEIR DAYS—AND WILL ONLY INCREASE WHEN CHARLES ASCENDS THE THRONE, MAKING CAMILLA QUEEN CONSORT. BUT THE COUPLE FIND AMPLE TIME TO ENJOY GRANDCHILDREN—AND LOTS OF LAUGHS

Charles and Camilla walk the beach in St. George's, Grenada, during a 2019 visit. "They are in a good place," former palace staffer Dickie Arbiter told *People* in 2018.

IT WAS THE FIRST TIME anyone from Buckingham Palace had made an official visit to Cuba since 1959—the year Fidel Castro took power. But with the goal of exploring cultural and academic connections between the U.K. and Cuba, Prince Charles and Camilla, Duchess of Cornwall, spent four days there in 2019, during a 12-day tour of the Caribbean. After a wreath-laying ceremony at Havana's Revolution Square, he visited a training gym for the boxers the small island nation is famous for, while she toured a maternity home. There was a meeting with Cuban president Miguel Diaz-Canel and an outing to the Grand Theatre Alicia Alonso. But the photo that went round the world was of the pair behind the bar at a Havana restaurant, gamely mixing their

Right: The couple's 2015 official Christmas card.

Opposite: Camilla playfully fanned her husband while at a Jodhpur, India, arts-and-crafts market as part of a 2006 tour of Egypt, Saudi Arabia and India.

Below: Charles and Camilla lose it to laughter while making artwork with children in Dulwich, England, in 2012.

own mint-sprigged mojitos and grinning at one another like giddy lovers on spring break.

At 71 and 72, respectively, Charles and the woman he has loved for nearly 50 years are thoroughly enjoying their happy hour. Since his father, Prince Philip, 98, retired from royal duties in 2017 and his mother, the Queen, 94, has pulled back somewhat, a more confident Charles has stepped into his role as the family's foremost ambassador, with the unflappable Camilla at his side. "He is a better person for having her, he's happier in himself," Camilla biographer Christopher Wilson told *People*. "And she has proved how good she is at being the wife of the Prince of Wales."

It is not always an easy calling. Charles has some 500 events per year on his calendar, supporting the many causes he is zealous about, including architectural preservation, youth opportunities and the environment. Camilla, who has more than 90 patronages of her own and often appears solo at events such as the Animal Care Trust and the Tetbury Film Society, "has risen to the challenge," says another insider. More than equal to her tasks, Camilla brings an evident joy to photo ops that have her feeding carrots to horses (she's a horse lover and rider) or sharing an ice cream with actress Dame Judi Dench (who wouldn't enjoy that?). "She has maintained her dignity and showed what a wonderful sense of humor she's got," Wilson says. "She's acquired, with difficulty, the polish of royalty but, importantly, has been there in a support role for Charles." Her good cheer is genuine, says friend Jilly Cooper: "She never grumbles."

These are tumultuous times for the future King. In November 2019 his brother Andrew was forced to stand down from royal duties after he gave a disastrous interview to the BBC about his ties to convicted sex offender Jeffrey Epstein. Soon after, Charles called for streamlining the monarchy—saying, effectively, that there were too many royals. What he probably did not expect is that the winnowing-down would start with his younger son Harry and daughter-in-law Meghan, who in January announced they planned to give up royal duties and in March officially left England and settled in Los Angeles with their son Archie. "Charles is a father, and he loves his son, but he is also thinking about the future of the institution," a palace expert told *People* at the time, calling a future without Harry in it "rubbish." Added another source: "Charles has always envisioned working with both of his sons and

their families." Personally, it may also be a painful loss, as both Charles and Camilla relish their roles as grandparents to Archie as well as to William's three children, George, Charlotte and Louis. Camilla's two grown children from her marriage to Andrew Parker Bowles have also made her a grandmother five times over. "I'd recommend it to everybody," she said in the 2018 documentary *The Real Camilla: HRH the Duchess of Cornwall*. "It's very nice because you haven't got the full responsibility. You can give them a wonderful time, spoil them, give them all the things their parents won't allow and then give them back again."

And when the time comes for her husband to ascend to the throne, she will most likely take another title: Queen Consort. Is Britain ready for a Queen Consort Camilla? In many ways, it would seem so. As she and Charles have now been married for 15 years, Camilla is front and center at royal weddings and christenings, in family portraits and official events. Last autumn she made a rare joint appearance with Queen Elizabeth—and without Charles present—at a ceremony marking 750 years since Westminster Abbey was rebuilt under the reign of King Henry III. What sort of Queen Consort will she be? By most guesses, rather approachable. "She has such an unstuffy way. There are no airs and graces about her," lauds British actor and author Charlie Higson, who chatted with the duchess at a 2011 event to promote literacy. And it is possible she will help determine how Charles will be as King. "She's made a massive difference in him," a longtime palace reporter told *Vanity Fair*. "He's much more relaxed now. They are always laughing and chatting; they have great affection and humor between them." The proof is when the two septuagenarians get their groove on, explained Camilla's nephew Ben Elliot. "They are both clearly great on their own. But two and two makes five in a big way here. They enjoy each other's company so much. You can see it best when they are dancing together—such genuine, deep-down affection and love. They both get the giggles—she first, then he tries to hold it together."

Opposite: Camilla joined Harry, Meghan and Kate in the ride to the annual Trooping the Colour, a celebration of the Queen's official birthday, in June 2019.

Left: Have we met? Charles looks on as Camilla happily tries out a one-person air-raid shelter as part of the 20th-anniversary celebration of the London Transport Museum in March.

Below: Camilla and Charles join William and Kate at a February visit to the Defence Medical Rehabilitation Centre in Loughborough, England, which provides assistance to disabled veterans.

HOW DIANA STAYS WITH US TODAY

KATE, A FUTURE QUEEN OF ENGLAND, TAKES MANY CUES FROM—AND OFTEN PAYS TRIBUTE TO—THE WOMAN WHO REDEFINED THAT ROLE

EVEN BEFORE DIANA'S untimely death at age 36, history had turned the page on her ever becoming Queen—her split from Charles decided that. But the way Diana did things, from hugging a child in a rope line to projecting modern British glamour on the world stage, stays with us. And that may be, in large part, thanks to another future Queen: Kate, Duchess of Cambridge, who often evokes the mother-in-law she never got to meet.

There are plenty of external clues as to how highly Kate regards her husband's mother: Diana's sapphire engagement ring, a constant on Kate's hand; the flowing light blue outfit Kate wore on a 2019 tour of India that was both an homage and a perfect modern update to one that

Above, left: Diana greeted a crowd in Florence in April 1985. Kate (above, with William) near Swansea, South Wales, in February 2020.

Diana had worn in 1996; the way they both perfected the "duchess slant," the art of sitting with one's knees and ankles together at an angle (for modesty and leg-lengthening's sake).

But it's the warmth and common touch, her devotion to work on behalf of children, that suggest Kate may become the kind of Queen Diana might have been. "Kate wants to be the People's Princess too," Ingrid Seward, editor in chief of *Majesty,* told *People.* "This is why she's been quite gentle in trying to find a role for herself, which she has now." For Kate, that means campaigning for mental health, a topic that was virtually taboo when Diana spoke of her postpartum depression and eating disorder. Though Diana was known for her work on behalf of AIDS victims and to rid the world of land mines, her "day-to-day unseen work was largely mental health-oriented," Patrick Jephson, Diana's former private secretary, told *People.* Noted Peter Fonagy, CEO of the Anna Freud centre, which supports mental health

Left: During a tour of Ireland in March 2020, Kate took the field for a bit of Gaelic football in Galway. Diana too was keen on sports.

Right: Kate (with William) wore a patterned Alexander McQueen gown to the 2020 BAFTA Awards, held at London's Royal Albert Hall.

Below: Kate visited cancer patient Beth Ansell, 18, during the September 2011 opening of the Oak Centre for Children and Young People in London.

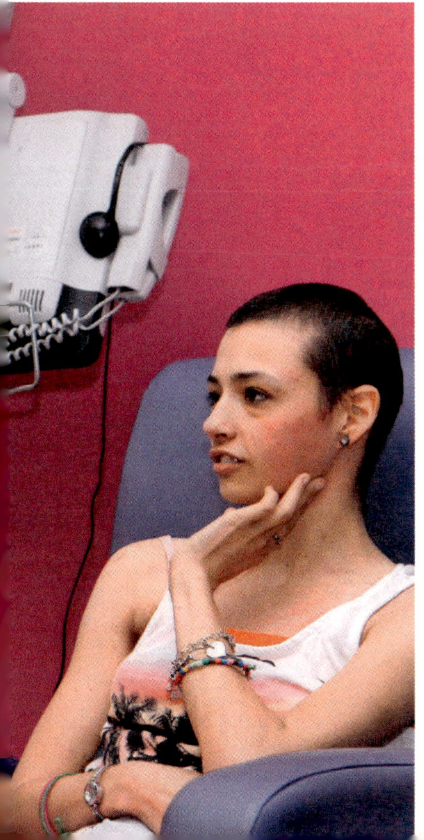

The parents of three (George, Charlotte and Louis, then 13 months, making his Buckingham Palace balcony debut in 2019) are hands-on and seem to thrill at the job.

initiatives for youth and families: Their patron Kate is "making the same critical contribution" as Princess Diana made about AIDS in terms of erasing stigma.

As a mum, Kate, like Diana, is liberal with hugs and kisses, radiates fun rather than a stiff upper lip, and is as determined as Diana was to see her kids raised outside the strict protocols of the past. "In many ways the royal family today is . . . what Diana always wanted. It's more inclusive, it's more touchy-feely, it's more accessible," says biographer Andrew Morton. Kate and Will are hands-on parents, sending George early to a Montessori school and as often as possible leaving Kensington Palace for the country, where she handles the baking and mandates plenty of outdoor time. "You can see Kate is a great mom," a source told *People*. "Clearly the kids are having fun." Adds historian Arianne Chernock: "The royal family owes a huge debt to Diana."

CREDITS

FRONT COVER
(Prince Charles & Duchess of Cornwall) Anwar Hussein Collection/Getty Images; (Princess Diana) from top) Jayne Fincher/Getty Images; Getty Images

TABLE OF CONTENTS
2-3 Peter Macdiarmid/Getty Images

THE WOMEN WHO SHOOK THE THRONE
4 Samir Hussein/Getty Images; 5 Bachrach/Getty Images; 6-7 Ken Goff/The LIFE Images Collection/Getty Images

ALL THE GIRLS HE LOVED BEFORE
8-9 Rolls Press/Popperfoto/Getty Images; 10 Shutterstock; 12 Serge Lemoine/Getty Images; 13 (from top) David Cole/Shutterstock; Desmond O'Neill; 14 Frank Barratt/Keystone/Getty Images; 15 (from top) Ray Bellisario/Popperfoto/Getty Images; Anwar Hussein/Getty Images; 16 (from top) Tim Graham Photo Library/Getty Images; Serge Lemoine/Getty Images; 17 (clockwise from bottom right) Serge Lemoine/Getty Images; Tim Graham Photo Library/Getty Images(2)

WHO'S THAT GIRL?
18 PA Images/Getty Images; 19 Bob Thomas/Popperfoto/Getty Images; 20 Tim Graham Photo Library/Getty Images; 21 (clockwise from top left) REX/Shutterstock; Fox Photos/Hulton Archive/Getty Images; Kypros/Getty Images; 22 PA Images/Getty Images; 23 Tim Graham Photo Library/Getty Images

SEALED WITH A KISS
24-25 Jayne Fincher/Princess Diana Archive/Getty Images; 26-27 PAWire/Zuma Press; 28 Reginald Davis/Shutterstock; 29 David Levenson/Getty Images; 30 (from top) Lichfield Archive/Getty Images; Princess Diana Archive/Getty Images; 31 Bob Thomas/Popperfoto/Getty Images

COME RAIN OR SHINE
32 Anwar Hussein/Getty Images; 33 Central Press/Getty Images; 35 Bob Thomas/Popperfoto/Getty Images; 36 Corbis/Getty Images; 37 PA Images/Getty Images; 38 Tim Graham Photo Library/Getty Images; 39 John Shelley Collection/Avalon/Getty Images(2); 40-41 Tim Graham Photo Library/Getty Images

THE PEOPLE'S PRINCESS
42-43 Jayne Fincher/Getty Images; 44-45 (clockwise from top) Anwar Hussein/Getty Images; Bob Thomas/Popperfoto/Getty Images; Jayne Fincher/Princess Diana Archive/Getty Images; 46 (from top) Tim Graham Photo Library/Getty Images; Anwar Hussein/Getty Images; 47 Tim Graham Photo Library/Getty Images

MORE THAN OLD FRIENDS
48-49 Anwar Hussein/Getty Images; 51 Sipa/Shutterstock; 52 (from top) Tim Graham Photo Library/Getty Images; Shutterstock; 53 Iain Burns/Camera Press/Redux

AIRING THEIR LAUNDRY IN PUBLIC
54 Corbis/Getty Images; 55 Getty Images; 56 Garcia/Gamma-Rapho/Getty Images; 57 (from top) Jayne Fincher/Getty Images; ITV/Shutterstock; 59 (from top) Steve Etherington/EMPICS/Getty Images; Shutterstock; 60 Anwar Hussein/Getty Images 61 (from top) Kent Gavin/Mirrorpix/Getty Images; Johnny Eggitt/AFP/Getty Images

MAKING THEIR OWN PATH
62 Corbis/Getty Images; 63 Samir Hussein/Getty Images; 64 Glenn Harvey; 65-66 Tim Graham Photo Library/Getty Images(2); 67 (from top) Tim Graham Photo Library/Getty Images; Stan Karczmarz/Getty Images; 68 J.L.Macault/MAXPPP/Zuma Press; 69 Robert A. Davis/AFP/Getty Images

OUT OF THE SHADOWS, BRIEFLY
70 Shutterstock; 71 Mark Cuthbert/UK Press/Getty Images; 72 Francis Silvan/AFP/Getty Images; 73 Julian Parker/UK Press/Getty Images; 74-75 Anwar Hussein/Getty Images

HAPPY AT LAST!
76-77 Richard Pohle/WPA/Getty Images; 78 79 Shutterstock(2); 80 Andrew Parsons - PA Images/Getty Images; 81 Antony Jones/UK Press/Getty Images; 82-83 Anwar Hussein/Getty Images

CHARLES AND CAMILLA TODAY
84-85 Chris Jackson/Getty Images; 86 (from top) Clarence House/Getty Images; John Stillwell/Getty Images; 87 MJ Kim/Getty Images; 88 Neil Mockford/GC Images/Getty Images; 89 (from top) Victoria Jones/Getty Images; Richard Pohle/WPA/Getty Images

HOW DIANA STAYS WITH US
90 De Keele/SOLA/Gamma-Rapho/Getty Images; 91 Ben Birchall/Getty Images; 92 (from top) Julien BehalPool/Samir Hussein/Getty Images; Kirsty Wigglesworth/Getty Images; 93, 94 Samir Hussein/Getty Images(2);

END
96 Tomos Brangwyn/Getty Images

BACK COVER
(from top) Jayne Fincher/Princess Diana Archive/Getty Images; Anwar Hussein Collection/Getty Images

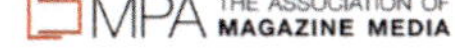

Copyright ©2020 Meredith Corporation
225 Liberty Street • New York, N.Y. 10281
All rights reserved. No part of this book may be reproduced in any form or by any electronic or mechanical means, including information storage and retrieval systems, without permission in writing from the publisher, except by a reviewer, who may quote brief passages in a review.
For syndication requests or international licensing requests or reprint and reuse permission, email syndication@meredith.com. Printed in the USA.

PEOPLE
Editor Dan Wakeford
Creative Director Andrea Dunham
Director of Photography Ilana Schweber
Director of Editorial Operations Alexandra Brez

PEOPLE BOOKS
Editor Allison Adato
Art Director Greg Monfries
Photo Editor C. Tiffany Lee
Contributing Photo Editor, Kali Abdullah
Writers Eileen Finan, Patrick Rogers, Lisa Russell
Deputy Art Director Ronnie Brandwein-Keats
Reporters Stewart Allen, Sue Carswell, Mary Hart
Copy Desk Joanann Scali (Chief), James Bradley (Deputy), Ellen Adamson, Gabrielle Danchick, Rich Donnelly, Ben Harte, Matt Weingarden (Copy Editors)
Production Designer Peter Niceberg
Premedia Trafficking Supervisor Chris Sprague
Color Quality Analyst Heidi Parcel

MEREDITH SPECIAL INTEREST MEDIA
Vice President & Group Publisher Scott Mortimer
Vice President, Group Editorial Director Stephen Orr
Vice President, Marketing Jeremy Biloon
Executive Account Director Doug Stark
Executive Publishing Director Megan Pearlman
Director, Brand Marketing Jean Kennedy
Associate Director, Brand Marketing Bryan Christian
Senior Brand Manager Katherine Barnet
Associate Director, Business Development and Partnerships Nina Reed

Editorial Director Kostya Kennedy
Creative Director Gary Stewart
Director of Photography Christina Lieberman
Editorial Operations Director Jamie Roth Major
Manager, Editorial Operations Gina Scauzillo

Special thanks Brad Beatson, Melissa Frankenberry, Sandra Jurevics, Samantha Lebofsky, Julie Mazziotta, Kate Roncinske, Laura Villano

PEOPLE Public Relations Marnie Perez, Julie Farin

MEREDITH NATIONAL MEDIA GROUP
President, Meredith Magazines Doug Olson
President, Consumer Products Tom Witschi
President, Chief Digital Officer Catherine Levene
Chief Revenue Officer Michael Brownstein
Chief Marketing & Data Officer Alysia Borsa
Marketing & Integrated Communications Nancy Weber

SENIOR VICE PRESIDENTS
Consumer Revenue Andy Wilson
Corporate Sales Brian Kightlinger
Direct Media Patti Follo
Research Solutions Britta Cleveland
Strategic Sourcing, Newsstand, Production Chuck Howell
Digital Sales Marla Newman
The Foundry Matt Petersen
Product & Technology Justin Law

VICE PRESIDENTS
Finance Chris Susil
Business Planning & Analysis Rob Silverstone
Consumer Marketing Steve Crowe
Corporate Communications Jill Davison
Brand Licensing Toye Cody and Sondra Newkirk

Vice President, Group Editorial Director Stephen Orr
Director, Editorial Operations & Finance Greg Kayko

MEREDITH CORPORATION
President & Chief Executive Officer Tom Harty
Chief Financial Officer Jason Frierott
Chief Development Officer John Zieser
Chief Strategy Officer Daphne Kwon
President, Meredith Local Media Group Patrick McCreery
Senior Vice President, Human Resources Dina Nathanson

Chairman Stephen M. Lacy
Vice Chairman Mell Meredith Frazier

To the world, they are the Prince of Wales and Duchess of Cornwall. To friends, Charles and Camilla. But to each other, they've long been Fred and Gladys, pet names lifted from *The Goon Show,* a BBC radio comedy cohosted by Peter Sellers that ran in the 50s with a reunion show in 1972, two years after the couple (above, in 2006) met. Gladys's catch phrase: "Yes, Darling."

Made in the USA
Middletown, DE
02 August 2020

14177311R00055